Open String Bow Workouts

for viola

book two

by Cassia Harvey

CHP376

www.charveypublications.com - print books
www.learnstrings.com - downloadable books
www.harveystringarrangements.com - chamber music

How to Practice This Book

The aim of the book is to **develop bow control technique and a clear, resonant sound**. To use this book most efficiently, **listen** to your playing **as carefully as possible**.

Goals:
Clean, clear starts: the bow should get the string vibrating at the very start of the note.
Connected tone: continuous sound for all non-articulated notes (notes without dots above or below them.)
Rich tone: your strings should vibrate as widely as possible for the entire length of the note.

Note: If you hear a break in the sound, a squeak, a scratch, a whistle, or a fuzziness to the sound, or if one part of a note is louder than another part, adjust your bow arm movement and try the same section again.

Some bow adjustments that can help the sound are:
*   **relaxed bow hold**.
*   **correct posture**.
*   **relaxed neck, shoulder, elbow, wrist, and fingers**.
*   **playing with straight bows** (parallel to the bridge.)
*   **balancing the arm** evenly across two strings when playing a double stop. If the arm is too high or low, one string will be louder than the other.
*   **continuous, even motion** at bow changes, aided by loose fingers and wrist on the bow. Listen to make sure your bow is not speeding up in anticipation of the bow change. Try not to make any extra noise as you change bows.
*   **adjusting the length of the bow** to fit the length of the note: whole and half notes need longer bows than eighth and sixteenth notes.
*   **adjusting the placement of the bow** to fit the length of the note:
    1. *longer notes* need *slower bows* and should be played slightly closer to the bridge (because there is more tension in the string, the bow is forced to move more slowly and sustained notes are possible without running out of bow.)
    2. *shorter notes* need *faster bows* and should be played closer to the fingerboard (because there is less tension in the string, it will vibrate quickly more easily.)

For beginning students, I assign one page each week. For intermediate students, I assign one page every two days. And for advanced students, I assign one page every day.

-*Cassia Harvey*

How These Bowing Exercises Can Help You

1. This book helps you **focus on the bow** by allowing you to listen to the exact sound your bow is creating and adjust the bow movement to make better sound. The notes of the left hand - even on scales or other predictable patterns - can distract you from truly focusing on and improving your bowing, so these exercises are only on open strings!

2. The book gives you **specific exercises to target and improve** your string crossing, bow articulation, and overall mastery of the bow. Smoother bow changes, better agility across strings, and a more resonant tone can result from playing these exercises.

3. These exercises are **an easy and efficient way to improve your viola bowing**! In only a few minutes a day, playing one or two of these exercises with intense focus and careful listening can help you achieve better tone in less time than just learning bowing through playing repertoire.

Bow Techniques Used in This Book

Staccato - sharply stopped bows

Use the first finger on the bow to "catch and release" the string with the bow. Allow the bow to move freely (and quickly) during a staccato note and then use the first finger to stop the bow completely at the end of the note.

Portato - gently stopped bows

Use the first finger on the bow to gently stop and start the bow on the string. You should hear an actual stop but it should be non-obtrusive so it can be used in less-aggressive music settings, such as slow movements and supporting parts in chamber music.

Spiccato - bouncing bows

- **play at the correct "magic" spot on the bow, which is often the balance point.**
- **play with a good, well-balanced bow hold.**
- **work to have a relaxed shoulder, elbow, wrist, and fingers.**
- **play with a shoulder to elbow to wrist slope (no "high elbows".)**
- **have your bow hair at the correct tightness - hair that is too loose won't bounce and hair that is too tight won't make tone in between the bounces.**
- **play at a good speed for bouncing - playing too slow or too fast won't allow bouncing.**
- **listen for a gentle, bouyant sound; if you hear a harsh sound, try using a little more bow on each bounce.**

Open String Bow Workouts for Viola, Book Two

Table of Contents

In this book, any note *not* marked with a dot should be played legato (smooth.)

On pages 1-33, notes with dots over or under them should be played staccato: a quickly drawn bow that starts and stops sharply.

Part One: Staccato

Workout No. 1

Cassia Harvey

staccato

Workout No. 2

staccato

Workout No. 3

staccato

(smooth)

Workout No. 4

Workout No. 5

Workout No. 6

Keep bow *on* the string during the rests.

Workout No. 7

Keep bow *on* the string during the rests.

Workout No. 8

Workout No. 9

Workout No. 10

Workout No. 11

Workout No. 12

(smooth)

Workout No. 13

Workout No. 14

Workout No. 15

Workout No. 16

Workout No. 17

**Keep bow on the string as
you change bows; no hops!**

whole bow

tip

whole bow

simile

Workout No. 18

Workout No. 19

Workout No. 20

Workout No. 21

Workout No. 22

staccato

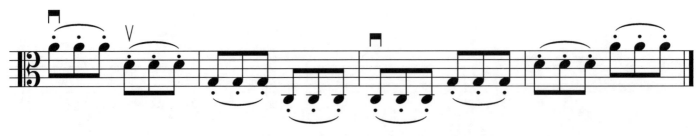

Workout No. 23

Workout No. 24

Workout No. 25

Workout No. 26

Workout No. 27

Workout No. 28

Workout No. 29

Workout No. 30

Workout No. 31

staccato

(smooth)

simile

Workout No. 32

Workout No. 33

Part Two: Dynamics

Workout No. 34

Workout No. 35

Workout No. 36

Workout No. 37

Workout No. 38

Workout No. 39

Part Three: Double Stops With Staccato

Workout No. 40

Workout No. 41

Workout No. 42

Workout No. 43

Workout No. 44

Part Four: Double Stops in Slurs
Workout No. 45

**Note: Use more bow on each note as you
crescendo and less bow as you decrescendo.**

Workout No. 46

Workout No. 47

Workout No. 48

Workout No. 49

Part Five: Grace Notes and Chords
Workout No. 50

Workout No. 51

Workout No. 52

These are played the same.

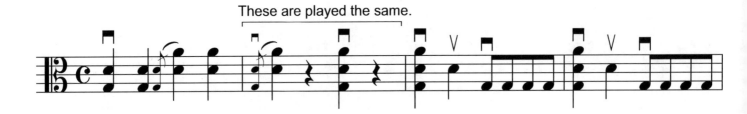

These two measures are played the same:
retake your bow after each chord.

These are played the same.

These two measures are played the same:
retake your bow after each chord.

These two measures are played the same.

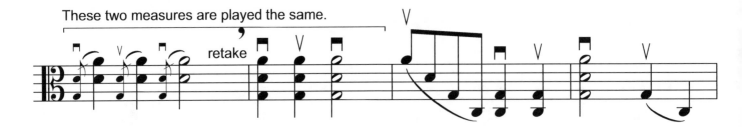

These two measures are played the same.

Workout No. 53

These two measures are played the same.

These two measures are played the same.

These two measures are played the same.

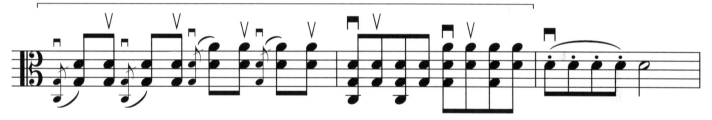

These two measures are played the same.

Part Six: Portato (Stopping the Bow Gently Inside Slurs)

Workout No. 54

Workout No. 55

Workout No. 56

Workout No. 57

Part Seven: Dotted Rhythms

Workout No. 58

Use the fingers and wrist, rather than the arm, to change bows in these next pages.

These two measures are played the same.

Workout No. 59

Workout No. 60

Workout No. 61

Workout No. 62

Part Eight: Hooked Bowing
Workout No. 63

Stop the bow to play staccato on the sixteenth note.

(smooth)

Workout No. 64

Workout No. 65

Workout No. 66

Workout No. 67

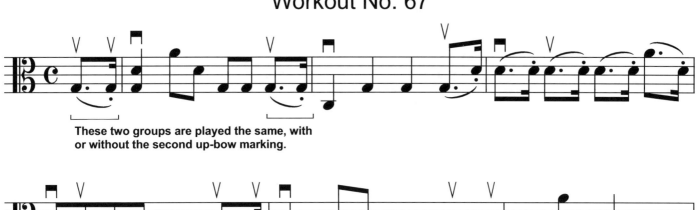

These two groups are played the same, with or without the second up-bow marking.

Part Nine: 6/8 Counting

Workout No. 68

Workout No. 69

Workout No. 70

Use the fingers and wrist, rather than the arm, to change bows in these next pages.

Workout No. 71

Workout No. 72

Workout No. 73

Workout No. 74

Workout No. 75

Workout No. 76

These two measures are played the same.

These two measures are played the same.

These two measures are played the same.

Workout No. 77

Workout No. 78

Workout No. 79

Part Ten: Single Bow Staccato

Workout No. 80

Staccato: Start the bow by catching the string with the bow and releasing. Move the bow quickly as you play the note. Then, stop the bow sharply on the string to end the note. Leave bow on the string during the rests.

Use **1/2 bow** for each note.

Use **3/4 bow** for each note.

Now, use a whole bow for each note! The first note should start at the frog
and the next note should start at the tip. Continue using **whole bows** on each note!
Your bow needs to move quickly across the string; imagine your bow as an arrow being shot!

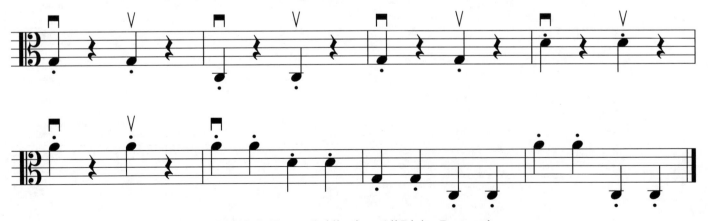

Workout No. 81

Use **1/2 bow** for each note.

Go to the middle of the bow for the next note.

Starting at the middle of the bow, play only in the upper half, from middle to tip, for these notes.

(Continue to play from middle to tip)

On pages 82-83, WB means whole bow, UH means play in the upper half of the bow (from middle to tip), and LH means play in the lower half of the bow (from frog to middle.)

Workout No. 82

Workout No. 83

Use a **whole bow** for each quarter note! Move your bow across the string as quickly as possible to reach the end of the bow!

Workout No. 84

Part Eleven:
Rhythmic Combinations

Workout No. 85

(smooth)

simile

tip

Workout No. 86

Workout No. 87

Part Twelve: Spiccato

Workout No. 88

Workout No. 89

Workout No. 90

Workout No. 91

Workout No. 92

Workout No. 93

Workout No. 94

Workout No. 95

Workout No. 96

Workout No. 97

Workout No. 98

Workout No. 99

Workout No. 100

Workout No. 101

Workout No. 102

Workout No. 103

Workout No. 104

Coda: Left and Right Hand Combinations for Rhythm

Workout No. 105

Note: These exercises can also be played on other strings.

Use any finger on the left hand to pluck the string (left-hand pizzicato.)

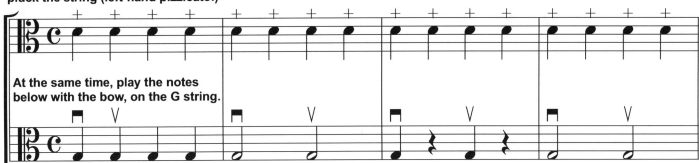

At the same time, play the notes below with the bow, on the G string.

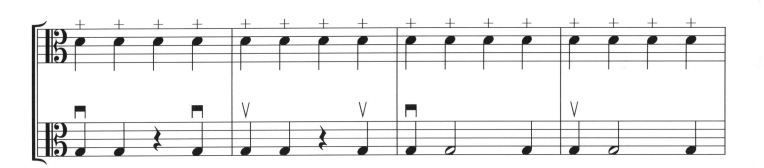

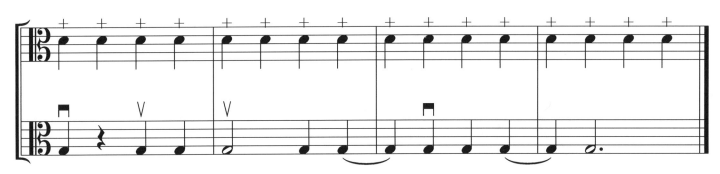

Workout No. 106

**Use any finger on the left hand to
pluck the string (left-hand pizzicato.)**

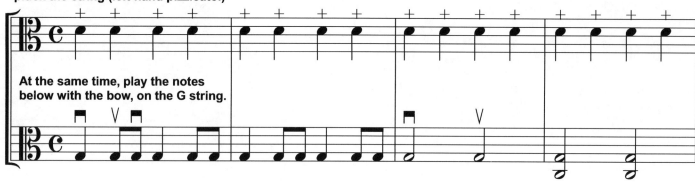

**At the same time, play the notes
below with the bow, on the G string.**

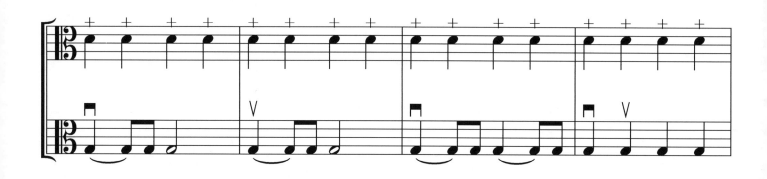

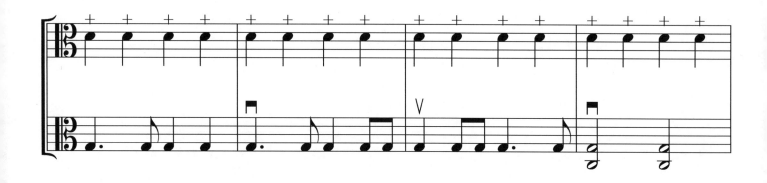

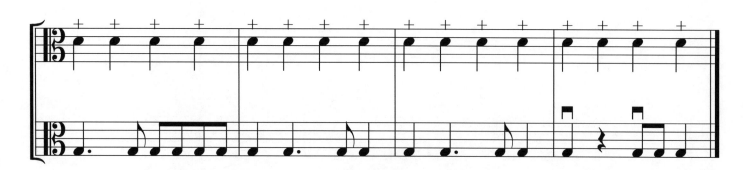

Workout No. 107

Use any finger on the left hand to pluck the string (left-hand pizzicato.)

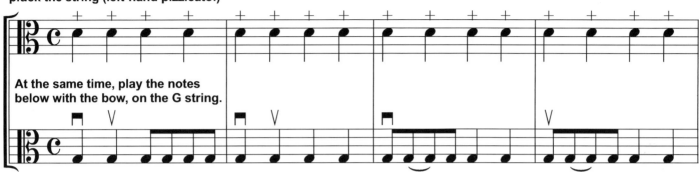

At the same time, play the notes below with the bow, on the G string.

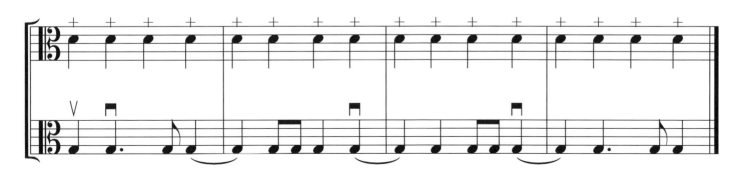

Workout No. 108

**Use any finger on the left hand to
pluck the string (left-hand pizzicato.)**

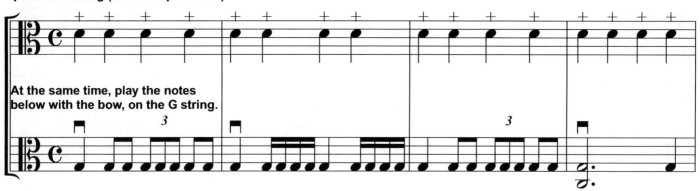

**At the same time, play the notes
below with the bow, on the G string.**

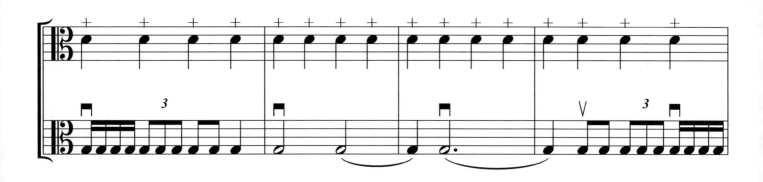

These two measures are played the same.

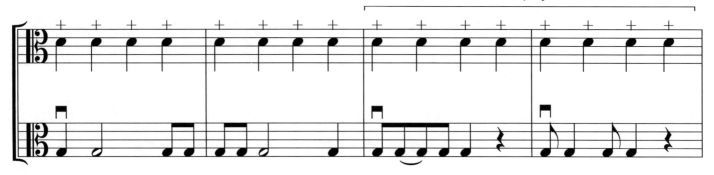

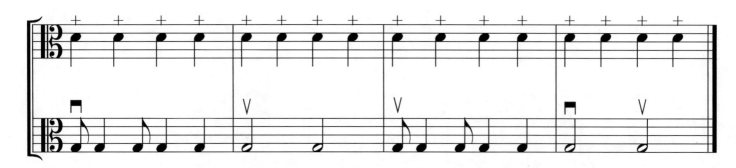

Workout No. 109

Use any finger on the left hand to pluck the string (left-hand pizzicato.)

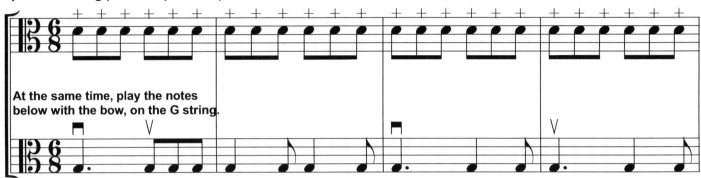

At the same time, play the notes below with the bow, on the G string.

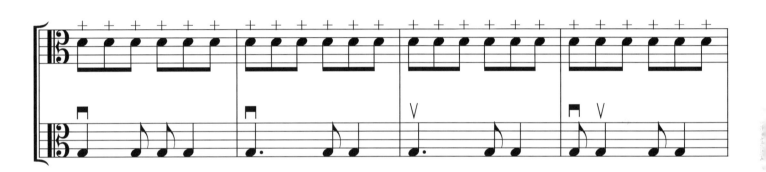

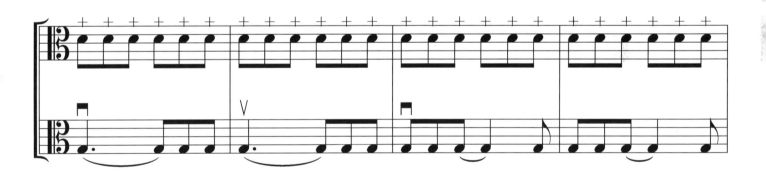

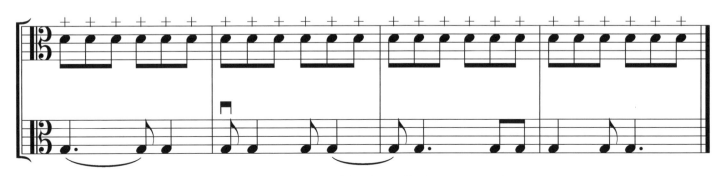

Workout No. 110

**Use any finger on the left hand to
pluck the string (left-hand pizzicato.)**

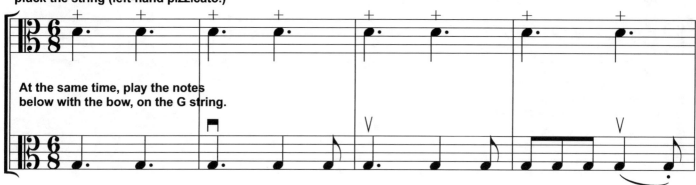

**At the same time, play the notes
below with the bow, on the G string.**

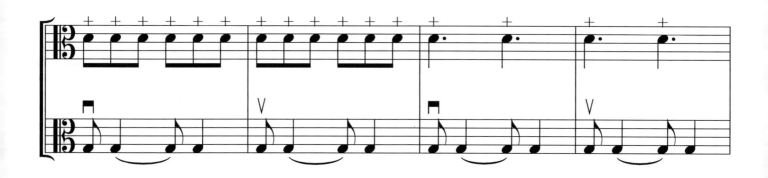

You Might Also Like:

Fiddles on the Bandstand: Fun Duets for Two Violas
Book One

all duets arranged by Myanna Harvey

Table of Contents

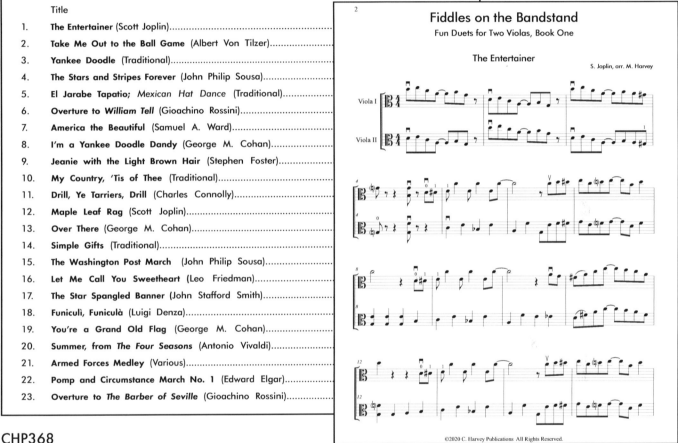

CHP368
$9.95   www.charveypublications.com

Take a journey to a simpler time when lawn chairs and blankets would be out under the stars and music would waft out from under the eaves of the wooden bandstand.

These are the tunes that got our feet moving, made us smile, and brought us together. Now, with these viola duets, you can bring the toe-tapping, exuberant joy to others and remind us all that through highs and lows, music can be something we share to keep our spirits up and build community.

From Scott Joplin to John Philip Sousa, these viola duets will invite you up on the bandstand, out for a gig, or out on your lawn to play your heart out! Know any violinists or cellists? You can pick up a copy of the violin or cello book and play with those instruments as well; the viola book is fully compatible with the violin and cello books.

This viola book is in first and third positions and is at an intermediate level.

Made in the USA
Middletown, DE
09 November 2024

63827665R00064